GODDESSES OF INDIA

Saraswati the Goddess of Wisdom

SHUBHA VILAS

Om KIDZ
An imprint of Om Books International

Once, the world was under construction by Lord Brahma. He had recently created all the planets but there were no laws yet in existence.

The planets had no idea whether they should rotate or revolve or make their orbits long or short. Since every planet moved as per its whims, there was utter confusion.

How do I manage this chaos? Brahma thought, absolutely bewildered. Regardless of what he created, there was no order. He had no idea how to bring sanity to the entire creation.

And then it struck him. He would create someone who had all the knowledge, wisdom and maturity to advise him how to bring order.

Excited and happy that he had found a solution, he sat down to meditate. Then, a magnificent personality emerged from his mouth.

She was Saraswati. Dressed in white, without any ornaments, she was seated on a swan radiating a soft glow. Her four hands symbolised Brahma's four heads. She held a palm leaf manuscript in one hand and a musical instrument (veena) in the other. Her other two hands held a rosary, and a pot of water. She was the Goddess of Knowledge. Mother of the Vedas. Inventor of Sanskrit.

Saraswati knew why Brahma had created her. Immediately, she put an end to the chaos. The melodious tunes of her veena had a profoundly soothing effect on the worldly commotion. Soon, the Sun, moon and stars came into existence and the world was organised into a sustainable pattern. The rivers and oceans became alive and the seasons swung into action. Everything fell into place.

Once, to rid the world from evil, Lord Shiva opened his third eye, and created a huge fire. Earth was on the verge of turning to ashes. The situation was so dangerous that Brahma asked Saraswati to become a river and save the world from the great fire. If Saraswati could become a river and deliver the ball of fire to the ocean, the threat could be aborted.

Saraswati did what Brahma asked her to do. She left Brahmaloka to reach sage Uttanka's ashram. Lord Shiva was waiting for her in the ashram to hand over the great fire called Vadavagni in a pot.

Saraswati held the pot firmly and transformed herself into a river. She flowed furiously with the intention of finding an ocean. She continued her journey till she finally immersed the pot in the ocean and saved the world.

Saraswati is the goddess of knowledge, speech, art and music. Saraswati expels the darkness of ignorance from the world.